THE STORY OF HOW I FOUND BIGFOOT

By H.E. Dawes Xist

This text is dedicated to all those who question and wonder... The truth has yet to be written.

TABLE OF CONTENTS

PREFACE

While the majority of this story is self-explanatory, I urge each reader to join the massive following that believes in Sasquatch and has seen it/him on many occasions. There is no certainty that on each venture you will see Bigfoot, but he is there, behind that branch, under that clump of moss...watching you.

YOUR JOURNEY BEGINS...

Tip: Silence is Key. Stealth is Golden.

Tip: Animals have a stronger sense of smell than humans.

Tip: Bring a compass.

SIGNS AND SIGNALS

Tip: To question is to discover.

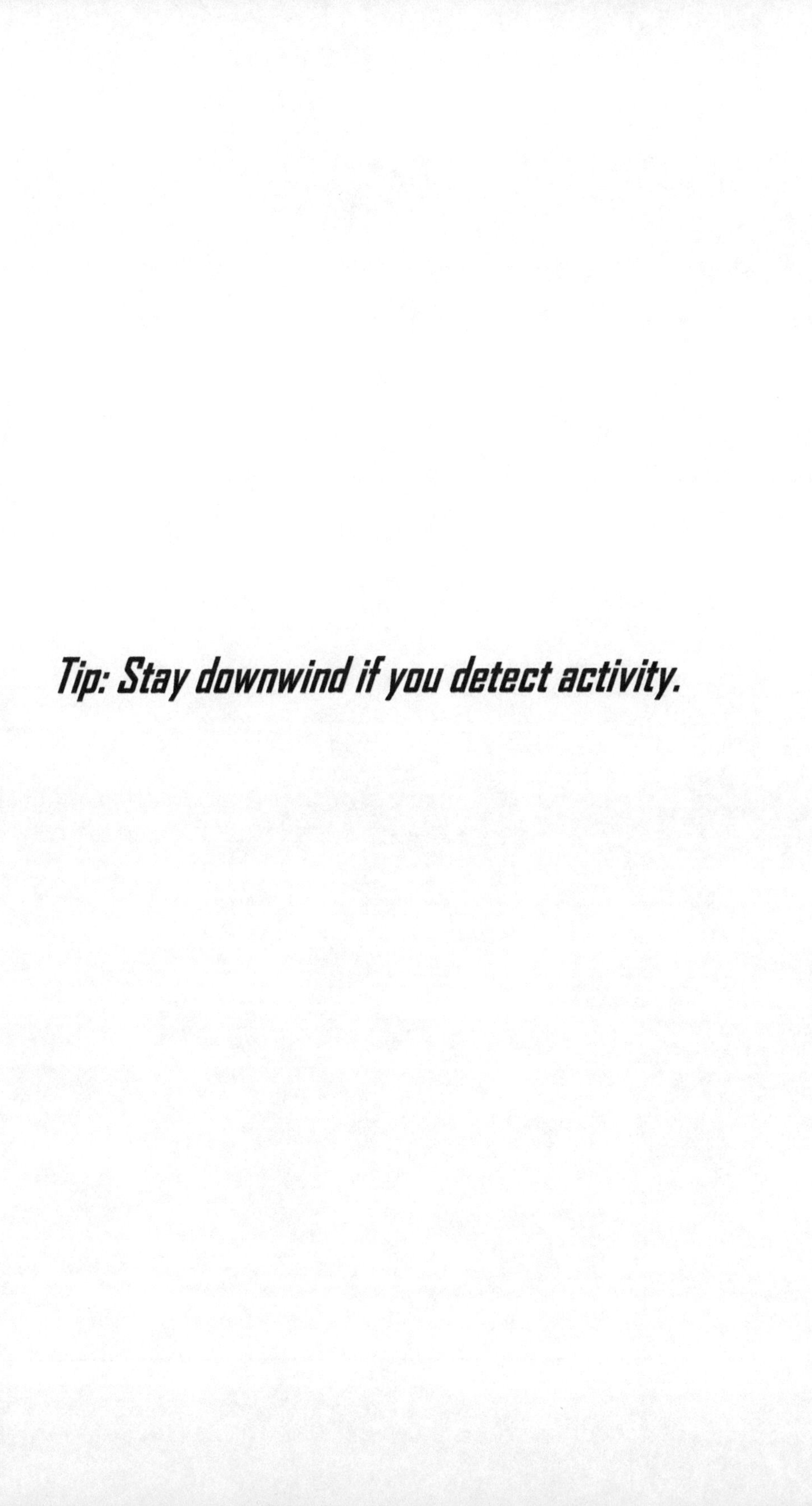

Tip: Stay downwind if you detect activity.

DANGER ON THE TRAIL

Tip: Sometimes it is just a feeling. Trust those hairs on the back of your neck and trust your instincts.

Tip: A human can live 7-10 days without food but only two days without water.

CARRY A BIG STICK

Tip: A walking stick has multiple uses.

Tip: Walk softly...

DISCOVERY

Tip: Look behind you!

Tip: Trees make noise when they move in the wind. But it is not always the trees that are making that noise.

TERROR FROM THE TREES

Tip: Remember to look up!

Tip: Do not be alarmed...until the birds stop chirping.

RUN!

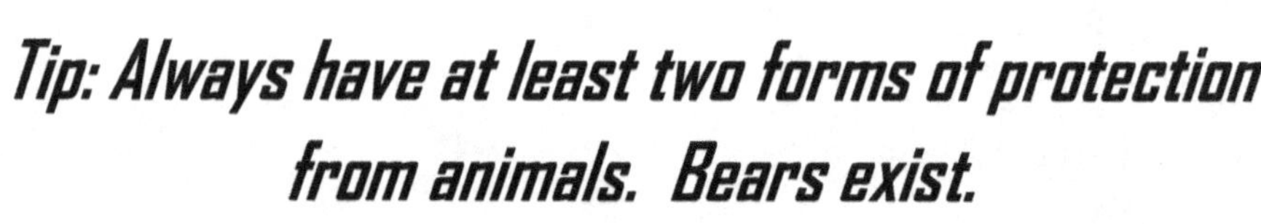

Tip: Always have at least two forms of protection
from animals. Bears exist.

Tip: Never go looking for Bigfoot without telling someone where you are going.

THE ENDING IS YOURS...

Tip: Keep a log of every crunch and every movement out of the corner of your eye.

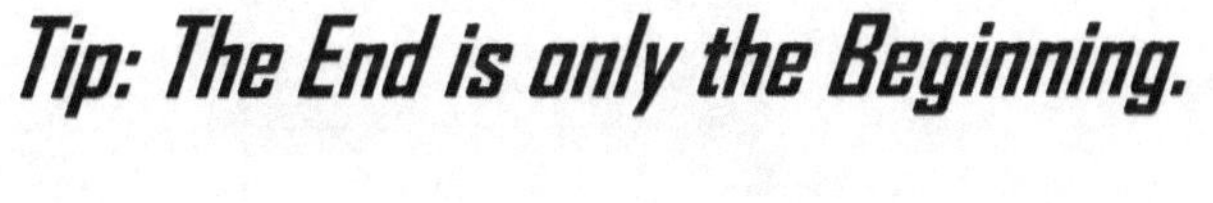
Tip: The End is only the Beginning.

Tip: Bring a camera.

AUTHOR'S NOTE

First off, I would like to state that I hope this manuscript serves as a useful tool to you on your hunt for Bigfoot and your ensuing fame and celebrity status. Secondly, I hope you continue the traditions set forth by the Bigfoot research committees who set out to prove, day by day, the existence of this marvelous creature. And last, I ask that if and when you do find Bigfoot, make first contact as peacefully as possible.

Thank you,

-H.E. Dawes Xist

www.ingramcontent.com/pod-product-compliance
Lightning Source LLC
Chambersburg PA
CBHW031423250726

48656CB00002B/797